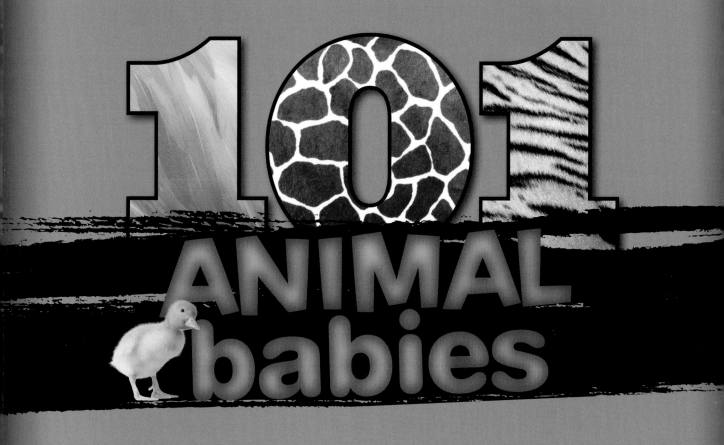

101 ANIMAL babies

ISBN 978-0-545-56321-5

12 11 10 9 8 7 6 5 4 3 2 1   13 14 15 16 17 18/0

Printed in the U.S.A.   40
First printing, September 2013
Book design by Kay Petronio

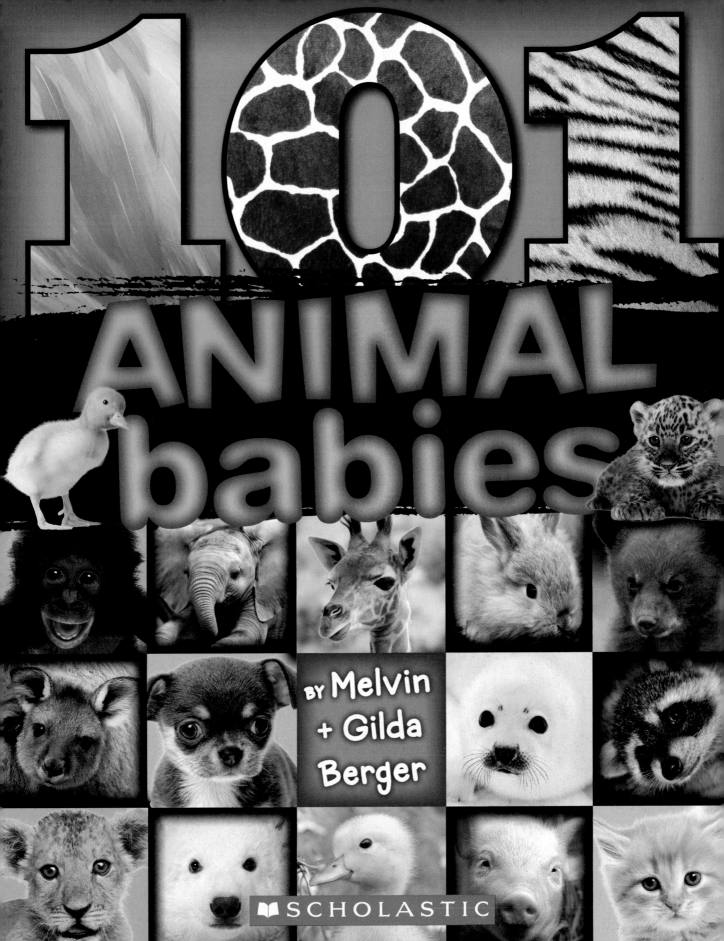

101 ANIMAL babies

BY Melvin + Gilda Berger

SCHOLASTIC

A female alligator lays from 20 to 60 eggs in a nest that she builds on the shores of a river, lake, creek, or marsh. She covers them with a layer of leaves and mud, and stays close by. After about two months, the mother hears the hatchlings call from inside the eggs. She uncovers the eggs just as the hatchlings are cracking open their shells. The mother then carries the newborns to the water in her huge mouth and watches over them for about a year.

#1 ALLIGATOR HATCHLINGS CALL FROM EGGS

#2 ANTEATER PUPS TRAVEL ON THEIR MOTHERS' BACKS

An anteater mom usually has one pup at a time. She carries it on her back for six months to a year and sets it down only when it's time to nurse. Since mom and pup are the same color, the pup stays hidden against mom's furry body. Once the pup starts walking, it will whistle loudly if left alone. By age one, the pup can find its own food, but continues to nurse for another year until it is fully grown.

An axolotl is an amphibian that stays an immature larva for life. Even so, an axolotl larva is much like any adult amphibian. Males and females mate and the females lay eggs that hatch into new axolotls. Since it is born in water and stays a larva, the axolotl breathes through gills and never grows lungs. As a result, the axolotl spends its entire life in water instead of dividing its time between land and water like other amphibians.

#3 AXOLOTL LARVAE STAY YOUNG FOREVER

#4 BABOON INFANTS CLING TO MOM

The mother baboon nurses her baby constantly for the first month of life. She holds it against her body with one hand while she leaves the other hand free to feed herself. As the baby grows bigger, it moves to her back, hanging on with its hands and feet. Mothers and babies set out each morning in large groups to find food. Young baboons sit upright on their mothers' backs until they're too big, at five or six months of age.

A female badger gets ready for the birth of her cubs in the spring. She makes a den in a burrow, or tunnel, deep underground. The cubs are born blind, deaf, helpless, and covered only with a thin layer of fur. For several months, the badger mother nurses and cares for her young all by herself. Gradually, the cubs start to wander out of the tunnel and eat solid food. By six months old, they leave the mother and den forever.

#5 BADGER CUBS ARE RAISED BY MOM ALONE

#6 BASS FRY DADS TAKE CHARGE

The male largemouth bass digs a nest in the river bottom with his tail. Then the female lays thousands of eggs inside that nest. Having laid the eggs, the mom swims away and leaves the dad in charge. He guards the nest and chases away predators, not even giving up his post to eat. The eggs hatch in just a few days. Then, tiny fry emerge and stay close to their dad for about a month before swimming away.

Bear cubs spend up to two years with their mother. She feeds them and keeps them safe from predators. The cubs follow their mom and she teaches them how to catch fish and hunt small animals. They also learn how to escape danger by climbing the nearest tree and staying away from large male bears that sometimes attack cubs. They imitate the calls their mom makes to keep in touch—especially when they get lost.

#7 BEAR CUBS LEARN SURVIVAL SKILLS

#8 BEAVER KITS LEAVE HOME BY AGE TWO

Baby beavers are called kits. They are born in cozy lodges, which are small houses built of branches and twigs in shallow water or along a river bank. The family includes the newborns, the one-year-old kits, the mother, and the father. Both parents feed and care for their offspring until they are two years old. Once they are two, the kits move out of the lodge to make room for new babies.

The beluga whale calf is born with dark gray skin that slowly turns white as it grows older. The first thing a newborn whale needs is a breath of air. Its mother and sometimes another whale may help it up to the surface. After that, the calf can breathe and swim on its own. The baby soon starts to feed on its mother's milk. It continues to nurse even after it learns to eat fish and shrimp. Mother and calf either swim together or join pods of other beluga mothers and calves.

#9 BELUGA WHALE CALVES CHANGE COLOR

#10 BOA CONSTRICTOR SNAKELETS ARE BORN ALIVE

Most snakes lay eggs that hatch into baby snakes, called snakelets. But one out of five species, including the boa constrictor, gives birth to live babies. As many as 60 babies are born at a time. Within a few days, they can protect themselves and hunt for mice and other small animals to eat. In time, boa constrictors grow to be about as long as a midsize car—up to 10 feet (3 m) in length.

Female butterflies lay their eggs on plants. But instead of hatching into baby butterflies, the eggs hatch into caterpillars! Each caterpillar eats the plant leaves and grows very fast, shedding its skin several times before reaching full size. The caterpillar slowly turns into a pupa (or chrysalis), with a hard outer shell. Inside, an adult butterfly slowly takes shape. When ready, a fully formed butterfly breaks out, flaps its wings, and flies away.

#11 BUTTERFLY CATERPILLARS HATCH FROM BUTTERFLY EGGS

#12 CAT KITTENS DOUBLE THEIR WEIGHT IN A WEEK

After a mother cat has kittens, she lies on her side and pulls the helpless babies toward her. The kittens drink her milk every two to three hours. In just one week they are twice their birth weight! After three weeks or so, the mother starts to spend more and more time away from her kittens. Without a steady supply of their mother's milk, the kittens begin to eat solid food. They wrestle and play, gradually getting stronger and faster. And they learn to stalk and attack—just like their wildcat relatives.

Most chameleon moms lay eggs in holes they dig in the ground. The eggs stay warm and moist and, most of all, they are safe from predators. The number of eggs the mother lays varies from about 4 to 100, depending on the kind of chameleon. The mom leaves after laying the eggs, and they hatch in about seven months. The young never meet their mom, but they are born fully developed, able to catch insects and avoid enemies.

#13 CHAMELEON HATCHLINGS CARE FOR THEMSELVES

#14 CHICKEN CHICKS CAN WALK, SEE, AND EAT AT BIRTH

Chicks hatch only from eggs that hens (females) lay after mating with roosters (males). The eggs hatch in 21 days. When a chick is ready to be born, it pecks a hole in the shell with the end of its sharp beak, known as the egg tooth. Then the shell breaks and the chick pushes out. The baby is covered with soft, fluffy feathers called down. Though just born, it can walk, see, and find its own food right away.

A chimp baby rides under its mother's body. The baby clings to her fur with its tiny fists while the mom nurses it. She also picks through the baby's hair with her long fingers to remove dirt and insects. By about six months, the baby chimp starts to ride on its mother's back. It rides with mom until it is about seven years old, with time off to play, search for food, and make a tree nest for sleeping at night.

#15 CHIMPANZEE BABIES STAY WITH MOM FOR YEARS

#16 CHINCHILLA KITS HAVE LONG, THICK FUR COATS

Chinchilla babies, called kits, are born covered by a layer of heavy fur that warms and protects them. If bitten or held by a fox, dog, eagle, or other predator, the kits have an excellent way to escape. They just let go of the clump of fur (called furslip) and flee without being harmed! Chinchilla babies also come into the world with their eyes wide open, which helps them spot predators and other dangers.

Female cougars have up to six cubs at a time. The cubs have spotted coats, with or without stripes, until they are six months old. Over the next two and a half years, the spots and stripes gradually disappear and the cubs turn a solid brownish-orange color. The mother raises her cubs alone, first feeding them milk and later meat that she has killed for them. After nine months, young cougars can hunt for themselves, but may stay with their mothers for up to two years while they look for homes of their own.

#17 COUGAR CUBS HAVE LARGE SPOTS ON THEIR FUR

#18 CRANE CHICKS FLY FAR

Cranes build dishlike nests in wet, open marshes or swamps. In the spring, a female usually lays two eggs in a nest and both parents care for the eggs until they hatch. In the fall, just a few months after the chicks are born, the entire flock, including chicks, flies south to a warmer climate. In the spring the flock heads back to its northern summer home. Crane chicks make these hundreds-of-miles-long journeys when they are only three or four months old!

When crocodile eggs are ready to hatch on land, the mother often takes a few of them into her mouth. She rolls the eggs between her tongue and the roof of her mouth, gently cracking open the shells. Next, she places the eggs on the ground and watches the tiny hatchlings break out of them. The mother gathers the hatchlings into her mouth and carries them down to the water. The hatchlings can swim and catch their own food right away. But mom guards them until they leave her at about five weeks of age.

#19 CROCODILE HATCHLINGS CAN SWIM

#20 CUCKOO CHICKS HATCH IN OTHER BIRDS' NESTS

Cuckoo birds are known for their calls and sweet songs. But a cuckoo mother is also very tricky. Instead of building her own nest, the female lays an egg in another bird's nest. As a result, foster parents raise the cuckoo chick! The foster chick actually pushes out any bird that belongs in the nest and eats its food.

In the spring, the mother deer usually has two fawns in a hiding place far from the herd. She nurses the fawns and licks them clean so they have no smell and predators cannot find them. The babies' spotted fur blends in with the ground, which also keeps them hidden. The mother leaves the fawns safe in the woods until they are strong enough to walk and follow behind her. The fawns stay with their mother for almost a year. She drives them off before she has new fawns.

#21 DEER FAWNS FOLLOW THEIR MOM

#22 DOG PUPPIES DEPEND ON MOM

Puppies are born tiny and helpless. Soon after birth, they begin to nurse and feed on their mother's milk for a month or more. By then they are ready to eat solid food that the mother spits up or finds for them. The puppies grow fast as they play-wrestle and chase one another. Most reach their full height by the time they're one year old. After the age of two, each year of a dog's life is equal to about five years of a person's life.

A dolphin mother takes excellent care of her calf for up to six years. But she doesn't do it alone. Relatives, called sitters, help her. Together, they lift the newborn calf to the surface to take its first breath of air. Sitters also care for the young while the mother is out feeding. Sometimes two or three females will swim in circles around several calves to keep the calves safe while they play!

#23 DOLPHIN CALVES HAVE BABYSITTERS

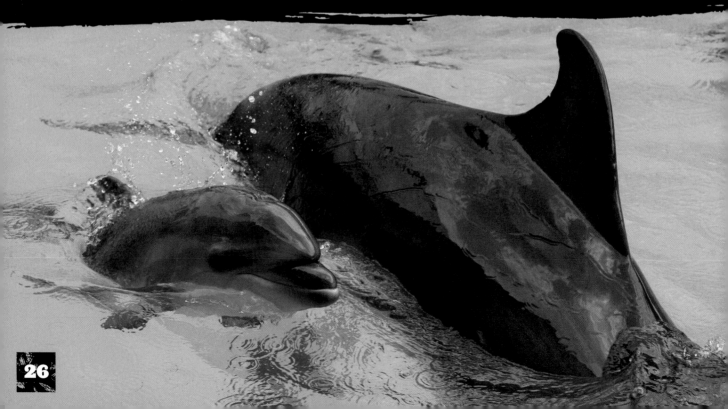

#24 DRAGONFLY NYMPHS LIVE IN WATER

Dragonfly nymphs hatch from eggs that the females lay on or near water. The newborns have no wings and do not fly. In fact, they don't look or act like their parents at all. Instead of flying, the nymphs live in the water for a long while, catching and eating almost anything that passes by. After between one and four years in the water, the nymphs climb out, sprout wings, and fly off as full-grown dragonflies.

Female ducks lay 6 to 12 eggs in shallow nests that they make on the ground. For the month or so that the mother sits on the eggs, the male watches out for predators. Soon after they hatch, the ducklings are ready to travel to water. They follow their mother as she leads them to a lake or pond. Dad waits and watches to make sure the young are safe. At about six weeks of age the ducklings are ready to fly off and live on their own.

#25 DUCK DUCKLINGS USUALLY HATCH ON LAND

#26 EAGLE EAGLETS HATCH IN HUGE NESTS

Eagles build gigantic nests at the top of trees near water. The female lays two or three eggs, which hatch in about 35 days. While the female keeps careful watch, the male hunts for fish or mice to bring to his family. The parents shred the meat with their beaks and feed it to the babies. The eaglets grow fast. Ten to thirteen weeks after hatching, the young are ready to fly.

Echidnas are one of the only two mammals in the world that do not give birth to live offspring. The female lays a single soft-shelled egg that she warms in a pouch on her belly. After 10 days, the egg hatches and a tiny baby, called a puggle, is born. For about three months, the puggle drinks pink-colored milk from a gland in the mother's pouch. The mother moves her baby to a burrow and returns every few days to feed the baby. When it is around a year of age and can care for itself, the baby leaves and never returns.

#27 ECHIDNA PUGGLES GROW FROM EGGS

#28 ELEPHANT CALVES SUCK THEIR TRUNKS

Elephant calves put the end of their trunks into their mouths, like human babies suck their thumbs. The calves also practice using their trunks for lifting and carrying things and giving themselves baths. Calves learn to drink by imitating the way their mothers suck up water with their trunks and squirt it down their throats. When starting to eat plants, calves even put their trunks into their mother's mouth, maybe to find out which plants she eats.

A male emu builds a shallow nest on the ground by himself. He lines it with leaves, grass, and bark. After one or more females lays eggs in the nest, the male sits on them for two months, night and day. He does not eat or drink during that time. If one of the mothers comes near, the father drives her away. Newborn chicks leave the nest when they're less than a week old. But dad continues to care for them for at least another six months.

#29 EMU CHICKS HAVE GREAT DADS

#30 FLAMINGO CHICKS LISTEN TO THEIR PARENTS

Mother and father flamingos "talk" to their eggs before they hatch, making high-pitched sounds next to the eggs. After the chicks are born, they remember the sounds and listen for them when their parents return from looking for food. The calls help the mom, dad, and chick find one another in the huge flamingo colonies in which they live. Chicks hurry to swallow the rich red drops of fluid their parents spit up for them. The fluid comes from the food the parents eat, which turns the chicks' feathers reddish.

A flounder fry is born with one eye on each side of its head, just like other fish. But as the fry grows, one eye starts to shift, or move, to the other side. By the time the fry has doubled its size, both eyes are on the same side of its body! The flounder now lives on the ocean bottom and its two eyes face upward, looking out for danger. Also, the top of the flounder's body is dark while the bottom is white, helping it to hide in the water.

#31 FLOUNDER FRY EYES CHANGE SIDES

#32 FOX KITS ARE BORN BLIND AND DEAF

Female foxes have litters of three to five kits that are helpless at birth. While mom nurses her kits and keeps them warm and safe, dad provides her with food. Mom eventually stops nursing by lying on her stomach at feeding time, forcing the kits to start hunting for their own bugs, birds, and mice. After several weeks, the kits begin to eat meat. Kits must also watch out for predators. Only one or two of the litter survive to adulthood.

Female frogs lay clumps of tiny eggs in water, and then leave. The eggs hatch in a few weeks and tiny fish-like tadpoles wiggle out. Over the following months, the tadpoles grow legs, their tails disappear, and they develop lungs for breathing air. The tadpoles have become adult frogs, able to live in water or on land. In two or three years, they are ready to head back to the water where they were born, and lay new clumps of eggs.

#33 FROG TADPOLES NEVER SEE THEIR PARENTS

#34 GIRAFFE CALVES RUN SOON AFTER BIRTH

A mother giraffe licks and sniffs her calf after it's born. Knowing her baby's smell will come in handy later when she has to find her calf among a large herd of giraffes. A giraffe calf is born able to stand and run. While very young, it joins a group of other giraffes, called a kindergarten. The calf plays with the others, stopping to nurse when the mother returns.

The two or three kids in a goat litter sometimes butt the mother's udder to get her to give them milk. Or they may butt to get others out of their way. Older kids butt one another to establish their place in the herd. Butting heads helps separate the leaders from the followers. When starting to eat solid food, kids butt to get the biggest portions. As adults they will butt heads to win the best mate, or to get almost anything else they need or want.

#35 GOAT KIDS BUTT HEADS

#36 GORILLA BABIES CRY

A baby gorilla is cleaned and groomed from the moment of its birth. The mother licks, picks, rubs, and nibbles every part of its body. Often, this makes the baby cry, almost like a human baby, as it kicks to get free. Sometimes, though, the grooming tickles the baby, which makes it chuckle! When done grooming, the mother feeds the baby her milk. Gorilla babies crawl at nine weeks and walk by nine months, which is a little faster than human babies.

In late summer or fall, female grasshoppers dig holes in the ground. Inside, they lay from 2 to more than 100 eggs. The following spring, the eggs hatch into a new generation of baby grasshoppers, called nymphs. During the next two months, the nymphs increase in size. They slip out of their old, hard, shell-like skin and grow new, bigger ones. After five or six changes, they are full-size adults, ready to hop about seeking plants to eat.

#37 GRASSHOPPER NYMPHS WRIGGLE OUT OF THEIR SKIN

#38 GUINEA PIG PUPS CUDDLE WITH MOM

Guinea pig pups are born with their eyes open and with a coat of fur. Soon after birth, they are able to run and play with the one to three others in the litter. They cuddle with their mother and follow her around for as long as six weeks as she feeds them her milk and later gives them solid foods to eat. Female guinea pigs are able to have babies at six weeks of age, but males are not ready to mate until they are 10 weeks old.

After her babies are born, the mother hare puts each one in its own shallow, grass-lined nest in the ground. She visits them once every night to give them milk and then hops away. While she is gone all day, the babies, called leverets, hide to keep safe from foxes and owls. When the mother returns, she gives a low call and listens for their answering calls. Hare leverets can live without their parents by only three weeks of age.

#39 HARE LEVERETS HIDE BY DAY

#40 HAWK EYAS EAT MEAT, JUST LIKE THEIR PARENTS

Most female hawks lay their eggs in nests high in the trees. The males help them care for the eggs until they hatch about a month later. The newborn hawks, called eyas, have a whitish, fuzzy covering, but no feathers for flying. They wait in the nests for their parents to feed them torn-up bits of meat, from bugs to worms to fish. As the young get bigger, they grow flight feathers. Around six weeks after the eggs hatch, the young birds fly away.

A female hornbill can lay between two and six eggs in the nest she makes in a tall tree hole. Then, using earth or mud and her own droppings, she seals up the hole and stays walled up inside. The male feeds his mate chewed-up insects and fruit through a narrow slit opening in the wall. When the chicks are half grown, the female breaks free of the nest. The young birds remain in the nest until they are adults with feathers. Then they, too, leave.

#41 HORNBILL CHICKS ARE BORN INSIDE TREES

#42 HORSE FOALS GROW QUICKLY

One baby (foal) is born to a female (mare) at a time—often at night. The mother licks the foal clean and dry, and gets to recognize her baby by its smell. Within an hour, the newborn is on its feet, taking its first steps, and looking for food. Most foals stay with their mom until they are four to six months old. They learn to graze grass and roam about freely. At the age of four years, a foal is considered a full-grown adult horse.

When hyena cubs are about a month old, their mothers move them to large community dens where they continue to nurse and protect them. Other hyenas in the group, or clan, visit daily with the cubs and their mothers. Hyena cubs generally drink their mother's milk for more than one year, which is far longer than cats or dogs, for example. At about two years, the male cubs join other clans and the females remain where they were born.

#43 HYENA CUBS NURSE LONGER THAN MOST MAMMALS

#44 IGUANA HATCHLINGS LIVE IN GROUPS

Female iguanas lay as many as 60 eggs at a time, which they bury in tunnels in the sand. About three months later, all the hatchlings break out of the eggs at the same time. The hatchlings leave the nest together, which protects them from predators. They stay in groups, sleeping with other iguana hatchlings on rocks or tree branches. Bands of young iguanas feed mostly on insects and snails, while adults eat plants.

A female jacana typically mates with as many as five different males. Each male builds a nest of plant material that floats on the water. When ready, the female lays a clutch of eggs in each nest. After laying the eggs, the female flies away, leaving the males to warm the eggs and care for the newborns. The downies are born able to swim, dive, and find their own food.

#45 JACANA DOWNIES ARE CARED FOR BY THEIR DAD

#46 JACKAL PUPS BABYSIT THEIR SIBLINGS

Adult jackals mate for life and form long-lasting family groups. Two to four pups are born at a time and eat food that their parents chew and spit out for them. The mother changes dens every two weeks to keep her young safe from attackers. At three months, the pups start to hunt for themselves, but their parents continue to feed them. Pups help raise their younger siblings by bringing them food or babysitting them.

Jawfish have huge mouths that hold the female's eggs until they hatch. The male jawfish has room for as many as 400 eggs in his mouth! When the eggs hatch, the male spits the babies, called fry, into the water. The young ones swim to the surface and start to feed. In a few weeks, they are ready to use their mouths to scoop out tunnels, or burrows, in the coral reefs where they live.

#47 JAWFISH BABIES' DADS HATCH THE EGGS

#48 KANGAROO JOEYS ARE THE SIZE OF BEES WHEN BORN

Just after birth, the tiny baby, called a joey, crawls into a pouch on its mother's belly—front feet and head first. The baby feeds on milk from a nipple inside the pouch for as long as nine months. Then it stops nursing, starts eating grass, and is ready to hop about on its own. Yet it stays close to its mother until about one year of age. When frightened, the joey rushes back and jumps into her pouch, where it is safer than being on the ground.

Koala joeys look like little bears, but they are related to kangaroos. A newborn koala makes its way into a pouch on its mother's belly, just like a kangaroo joey. Once inside, the joey attaches itself to its mother and drinks her milk for about six months. The baby leaves the pouch around then, usually by falling out the first time! But it comes back to nurse for some months before starting to live on its own.

#49 KOALA JOEYS ARE COUSINS TO KANGAROOS

#50 KOMODO DRAGON HATCHLINGS CLIMB TREES

Huge female Komodo dragons lay between 15 and 30 eggs in leafy nests on the ground. About nine months later, the eggs hatch, and the mother leaves. The newborns now make their way alone in the world. To avoid predators, the hatchlings climb into the trees and feed on insects and lizards. When they become too heavy for the branches, around four years of age, they come down to hunt larger prey.

Baby lemmings can mate as young as three weeks old. The mother carries her unborn for just three weeks and can get pregnant three or four times a year. Even more amazing, each litter can have as many as 13 babies! Because so many lemming babies are born so quickly, the population sometimes grows overly big in places where these animals live. When that happens, masses of lemmings sweep into new territories.

#51 LEMMING BABIES REPRODUCE VERY QUICKLY

#52 LEOPARD CUBS MOVE FREQUENTLY

For the first two months of their cubs' lives, leopard mothers keep taking them from one hiding place to another. Even when grown, leopards seldom stay in one place for more than two or three days. Mothers start training their cubs as hunters through play. Often, they flick their tails in front of the cubs, who try to catch them. The cubs also chase and pounce on their brothers and sisters. By one year of age, the cubs are first-rate predators.

Lionesses usually nurse their cubs for the first few weeks of life. After that, mom carries the cubs in her jaws and joins other mothers and cubs. The cubs now also get milk, protection, and care from other mothers. Around seven months of age, the babies may get their first taste of meat from members of the pride returning from a hunt. But it is not until they are about two years old that they begin to hunt for themselves.

#53 LION CUBS TAKE MILK FROM MANY MOMS

#54 LLAMA CRIAS ARE NOT LICKED BY MOM

Crias, Spanish for "babies," are baby llamas. But unlike many other mammals, the females do not lick their newborns clean. That's because their tongues are too short! Instead, the mother nuzzles and hums to her newborn. In time, the baby learns to nuzzle and hum back. Until it is one year old, the cria is very well cared for by the herd. When threatened, it calls out and someone comes running.

Meerkats live in large family groups of up to 50 members, called a gang. Females give birth to pups in underground tunnels, or burrows, with many entrances and exits. The newborns have little fur and their eyes are closed. For about two weeks they stay in the burrow, drinking mother's milk. After that, group members help care for and protect the young while their mother leaves to hunt for insects and other food.

#55 MEERKAT PUPS LIVE IN GANGS

#56 MOURNING DOVE SQUABS SOUND SAD

Mourning dove babies, called squabs, are named for their soft, sad calls. The young later use this call to find mates, with whom they stay for life. A female mourning dove usually lays two white eggs at a time. The newborns feed on a rich fluid, called crop milk, which they take from their parents' throats. The babies drink crop milk for three to four days, and then begin to eat seeds. At about two weeks of age, they are strong enough to fly away.

Mouse babies are born in nests made by their mother from rags, paper, or other soft material. The newborns have no fur and are deaf and blind. Because of their coloring, they are called pinkys. But the babies grow fast, and in about 10 days have full coats of fur and can hear and see. The mice squeak to one another in the nest and use smells to keep in touch, until they leave the nest in about three weeks.

#57 MOUSE PUPS ARE PINK AT BIRTH

#58 OCTOPUS BABIES RAISE THEMSELVES

A female octopus takes good care of the strings of eggs—up to 100,000—that she lays. She guards them against enemies and blows water across the eggs to keep them clean. Shortly after the eggs hatch, though, the mom dies. The babies drift up toward the surface of the ocean, where they spend many weeks, feeding on tiny living creatures. When bigger, they swim down to the ocean bottom, where they stay the rest of their lives.

Opossums are born with as many as 20 brothers and sisters. A newborn opossum is the size of a peanut. Called joeys, the baby opossums climb up their mother's fur and into her pouch. The pouch has about 13 teats, or nipples, but only 10 or so babies attach themselves and nurse. The other joeys die. After 10 weeks, the joeys leave the pouch and ride on their mom's back as she hunts for food. Three months later they go off on their own.

#59 OPOSSUM JOEYS ARE THE SIZE OF A PEANUT WHEN BORN

#60 ORANGUTAN BABIES HAVE LONG CHILDHOODS

Baby orangutans stay with their mothers for about eight years—the longest childhood of any ape! Father orangutans do little or nothing to help bring up the baby. Every day, the mother builds a special tree nest for herself and her single offspring, and feeds it fruit that she finds in the jungle. Over the years, the young orangutan acquires many skills by copying mom, from finding food and avoiding danger to getting along with other orangutans.

An ostrich egg is the largest egg in the world today—almost as big as a cantaloupe. Two or three females lay about 10 eggs in the same nest. Since ostriches are the biggest of all birds, one ostrich can sit on many eggs at a time. Males sit on the eggs at night and the females sit during the day. The eggs hatch in about six weeks. The chicks grow fast: a foot (30 cm) a month until they are seven or eight months old.

#61 OSTRICH CHICKS HATCH FROM SUPERSIZE EGGS

#62 OVENBIRD CHICKS HATCH IN CLAY NESTS

Ovenbirds take their name from the covered, oven-like nests that they build of clay and dry plants. The female ovenbird lays between three and five eggs in the nest, which protects them from predators and also keeps them very warm. The eggs hatch quickly in the cozy nests. The chicks grow their feathers in about 18 days, but they stay with their parents for up to three months.

A female owl takes about a month to hatch the 2 to 12 eggs she lays. The owlets are born with a thick white down and with their eyes closed. It may take them as long as two months to learn how to fly. But the parents never stop caring for them. With claws extended, they dive-bomb enemies, or distract approaching predators. Finally, though, the parents end the long period of care by chasing the owlets away from the nest.

#63 OWL OWLETS HAVE CARING PARENTS

#64 PANDA CUBS GAIN WEIGHT FAST

A newborn panda cub is smaller than a human thumb and needs its mother's full attention to survive. For two years, the mom stays close to the cub. She feeds it her milk, up to 14 times a day, for about three months. After that, she nurses it less often as the cub gets teeth and starts to eat bamboo. The cub grows quickly and in just one year goes from weighing a few ounces (grams) to the weight of an average third grader!

A peacock family includes a peacock (dad), a peahen (mom), and peachicks (babies). The peahen lays three to six eggs in a shallow ground nest and the chicks are born in a month. Right away, they can walk and search for food. In two weeks, their wings are strong enough for them to fly. At two months old, females look like their mom—but half the size. Males have their full display of feathers by three years of age.

#65 PEACOCK PEACHICKS FLY WHEN TWO WEEKS OLD

#66 PELICAN CHICK EGGS HATCH IN ABOUT A MONTH

Pelican parents take turns warming the chick eggs under their big, webbed feet. The eggs hatch in about a month and the chicks stay in the nest for another month or two. For the first 10 days, the newborns eat fish that their parents eat, spit up, and leave on the bottom of the nest. After that, the chicks take the half-eaten fish from their parents' huge bills into their own bills. By the end of two months, the young birds are ready to leave the nest.

Female emperor penguins leave the water to lay their eggs and raise their young on land. The mother lays a single egg on the polar ice and rolls it onto the broad, flat feet of the waiting father. He keeps it warm while she heads to the ocean for food. For about two months, the father warms and protects the egg until it hatches. The parents then take turns going fishing and caring for the chick. As all the chicks get older, the adults gather them into tight groups to huddle and keep one another warm.

#67 PENGUIN CHICKS HUDDLE TO KEEP WARM

#68 PIG PIGLETS FIGHT WITH THEIR SIBLINGS

Female pigs usually have between 8 and 12 piglets at a time—but sometimes only the greediest survive. That's because the nipples, or teats, near the mother's head produce much more milk than those near her tail. The biggest and strongest piglets get the teats that give the most milk. The weakest pigs drink from the teats with less milk, and so they don't grow as well. Most pigs double their weight in a week and reach 300 to 700 pounds (140-300 kg) when fully grown.

For the first week of life, pigeon parents feed their squabs a whitish liquid from their necks. It is called pigeon milk, or crop milk. The squabs open their bills and the parents squirt the milk down their throats. The young soon start to eat more and more solid food every day, finally stopping the pigeon milk after about 10 days. Six to eight weeks after hatching, the young fly away to mate and have their own young.

#69 PIGEON SQUABS DRINK PIGEON MILK

#70 PLATYPUS PUGGLES HATCH FROM EGGS

Unlike most mammals, platypus babies hatch from eggs. The female lays the eggs in a nest she digs in a riverbank, away from her mate. She warms the eggs for about two weeks against her curled-up body and doesn't leave until the eggs hatch. She also waits until the puggles have learned to suck the milk that oozes out of large pores in the skin under her body. In no hurry to leave, the babies stay in the nest for about four months.

Female polar bears dig homes in the snow before their cubs are born. The dens face south to keep them warm. Mom has from one to three small cubs in the middle of winter that she nurses for about four months. When spring arrives, the mother polar bear moves the cubs out of their snow home. The young stay with her for two to five years, learning how to survive in the Arctic and hunt seals, their favorite food.

#71 POLAR BEAR CUBS ARE BORN IN DENS

#72 PORCUPINE PUPS GROW QUILLS

In the spring, a porcupine mother gives birth to a baby, called a pup or porcupette. The newborn has soft hair bristles that become stiff quills in a few days. For the first six weeks, the pup drinks mother's milk and also eats plants. The pup travels with its mother through the summer and plays on the ground while she gathers bark, leaves, and twigs from the trees. By winter, though, the pup is independent of its mother. When threatened, the young porcupine raises, spreads, and rattles its quills.

Newborn prairie dogs spend their first six weeks of life in underground burrows, called towns. Each town is split into family groups made up of one male, a few females, and their pups. While mom nurses and cares for her litter of one to six pups, dad watches out for predators. The family helps out by sharing food, standing guard, chasing enemies away, and grooming one another. They kiss and nuzzle, but bark to signal danger.

#73 PRAIRIE DOG PUPS LIVE IN TOWNS

#74 PUFFIN PUFFLINGS HATCH ON LAND

Puffins are birds that live in cold Arctic waters. Early in the summer, though, they fly to land to start a family. Pairs of puffins use their beaks to dig long, narrow nesting burrows in cliffs along the coast. Inside, the females lay a single white egg. The egg hatches in about six weeks, and about six weeks later the newborn puffling flies off to fish in the water. Five to six years after that, the young bird heads back to land to have pufflings of its own.

A python mother forms her body into a coil around her soft, leathery eggs to keep them warm. If the weather turns cooler, she rapidly shakes her body back and forth, or shivers, which raises the temperature. For about three months, the mother snake stays coiled around the eggs, without eating, and only leaves for an occasional drink of water. Finally, the eggs hatch—and she leaves the snakelets to face the world alone.

#75 PYTHON SNAKELETS HAVE SHIVERING MOMS

#76 RABBIT KITS MULTIPLY FAST

Most rabbit kits are born in shallow nests or burrows. The three to eight kits in a litter have no fur and are blind at birth. By about one month of age, however, they are ready to hop away on their strong back legs. As early as two months later, they can mate and produce kits of their own. One female may mate six times a year. From one spring to the next, as many as 1,000 kits can be born, as her babies have babies, and so on and so on!

Before giving birth in the spring, the raccoon mother builds a nest in a quiet, covered den. A litter usually consists of two to five helpless young. The cubs don't leave the den for about eight weeks, as the mother hunts at night for insects, fish, frogs, or fruit to feed them. A few weeks later, the cubs follow their mother, slowly learning how to find their own food. They usually stay with mom until the following spring, when they leave to start a life on their own.

#77 RACCOON CUBS ARE DEAF AND BLIND AT BIRTH

#78 RHEA CHICKS HAVE BOSSY DADS

Rhea dads do everything for their chicks, from building the nest to protecting them. The moms have only one job, which is to lay the eggs! As many as 12 females lay eggs in a nest that can hold up to 60 eggs. The dad warms the eggs for about six weeks, chasing away any female rhea that comes too close. All the chicks are born within 36 hours of one another and the new dad drives away any rhea or other animal that threatens them.

Even though an African rhinoceros calf is born without horns, they start to grow them soon after birth. Within an hour of being born, the calf gets up on its wobbly legs and starts to drink its mother's milk. It may nurse for up to two years and forms a very strong bond with its mom. The baby rarely leaves her sight and usually remains with her until she is ready to give birth once more. The calf's horns continue to grow bigger throughout its life—sometimes as much as 3 inches (8 cm) a year!

#79 RHINOCEROS CALVES GROW HORNS

#80 SANDGROUSE CHICK DADS CARRY WATER

Sandgrouse chicks grow up in dry desert areas. Getting enough water is always a problem. That's when dad comes to the rescue. He flies off to a watering hole and soaks his breast feathers in the water. These special feathers draw up and hold the water while he flies back to the nest. The chicks, as well as mom, drink the water from his feathers. When they are two months old, the young can fly to the watering hole by themselves.

The first thing a newborn sea lion hears is its mother's trumpetlike call. The pup learns to answer its mother with calls of its own. Soon, the mother and pup get to recognize the sound of each other's voice. From time to time, the mother leaves to find food and the pup stays with a group of many other pups. When she returns, her special call and the pup's response quickly bring them together.

#81 SEA LION PUPS "TALK" WITH THEIR MOM

#82 SEA OTTER PUPS EAT WHILE FLOATING

A sea otter pup rests on its mom's belly after it is born. At about a month old, it starts to follow and imitate its mom. The young sea otter practices swimming and diving into the water to find food. Next, it learns to nurse, groom, and eat while floating on the water. It gathers clams, crabs, and mussels on the ocean bottom, just like its mother, and breaks open the shells with a rock to eat the animals inside.

Sea turtle mothers lay their eggs at night in holes they dig on sandy beaches. The mothers cover the eggs with sand and return to the sea. In about two months, the hatchlings break out of their shells. Working as a group, the hatchlings dig out of the nest and run as fast as they can to the sea, trying to escape waiting crabs, birds, dogs, or raccoons. Once in the water, they have only two predators—sharks and humans.

#83 SEA TURTLE HATCHLINGS DASH TO THE SEA

#84 SEAHORSE FRY HATCH ON DAD'S BELLY

A female seahorse deposits her eggs in a pouch on the front of a male's body. The number of eggs varies from about 50 to 1,500. The dad keeps the eggs in his pouch until they hatch, which can be from one to six weeks. The fry then leave the pouch one at a time through a small opening. The dad's work is finished as the newly hatched fry swim away in search of their first meal.

Most seal pups are born on land, even though seals spend most of their time in the water. The pup feeds on its mother's milk for as long as six weeks. The milk is very rich and the seal pup grows very quickly. By the time it has stopped drinking mom's milk, the pup has doubled its birth weight. As soon as the young seal learns to swim, dive, and hunt for fish, it is on its own. Mom then mates again and nearly a year later gives birth to another pup.

#85 SEAL PUPS ARE USUALLY BORN ON LAND

#86 SHEEP LAMBS GUZZLE MOTHER'S MILK

In the spring, mother sheep, called ewes, give birth to one or two lambs. The lambs can stand and walk within a half hour of being born. Soon, they begin to nurse milk from their mother. At first, lambs nurse very often—up to twice an hour. By the fifth week, they nurse once every two hours. The lamb and ewe get to know each other's smell and voice, making it easy to find one another even in the largest flocks.

The female shrew has between two to four litters of babies a year. She gives birth in a small, cup-shaped nest of leaves and grass, often under a rock. If an animal threatens the nest, the mother moves the babies single file to a new spot. Each baby follows mom with its teeth lightly grasping the tail of the baby in front. The babies grow up fast and at one month of age leave the nest. Most go on to have babies of their own later in the same year.

#87 SHREW BABIES WALK IN SINGLE FILE

#88 SKUNK KITS CAN FIGHT OFF DANGER

Skunk kits are born blind, deaf, and hairless. But even before they can see or hear, they have a powerful way to defend themselves. Kits as young as eight days can lift their tails into the air and squirt out a smelly fluid. It travels only a few feet but can be smelled much farther away. The scent is so horrible that most enemies learn to stay away. After two to three months, the kits leave to find their own way in the world.

A sloth mother gives birth to her baby in a tree, while holding on to a branch with her long, curved claws. The baby sloth clings to its mother's belly and drinks her milk for about a month. Around the second month, the baby rides on its mother's back while she moves among the trees of the forest. When mom hangs upside down, the baby rests on her belly. By nine months of age, the young sloth is ready to move about the trees alone.

#89 SLOTH BABIES HANG FROM BRANCHES

#90 SPARROW CHICKS EAT INSECTS, NOT SEEDS

Sparrow parents usually feed their chicks insects and spiders, while they themselves mostly eat seeds. After hatching, the mom and dad bring the newborns bugs to eat for about 10 days. When the chicks get their feathers and can fly, the mother leaves to begin her next family. But the father continues feeding the chicks for two weeks more, gradually switching from insects and spiders to seeds.

Female spiders lay hundreds or even thousands of eggs in tiny, silken egg sacs. The mothers either hide the sacs in webs or carry the sacs with them. It can take many weeks for the eggs to hatch into baby spiders, called spiderlings. The spiderlings get bigger, shedding their skins several times and growing new ones. When full-grown, the spider successfully uses its eight legs and pair of fangs to catch its insect prey.

#91 SPIDER
SPIDERLINGS NEVER MEET THEIR DAD

#92 SQUIRREL PUPS CHANGE NESTS

A female squirrel usually gives birth to three or four pups in the spring. Mother stays in the tree nest with her babies for 6 to 10 weeks. But sometimes she fears that a predator may find her and her pups. Or she cannot find enough acorns or other seeds for her young. Then the mother squirrel carries the pups in her mouth to a new home.

Swan babies, called cygnets, are born covered with soft brownish-white feathers. Only one day after they hatch, the cygnets are able to swim and dive in the water. Both parents feed and protect the young for the first weeks of life. Sometimes the cygnets go for rides on a parent's back. The cygnets grow fast and by the age of five months can fly. When they are about one year old, the parents force them to leave and make room for the next brood.

#93 SWAN CYGNETS HAVE CLOSE FAMILIES

#94 SWIFT CHICK PARENTS MAKE NESTS WITH SALIVA

Swifts build nests in chimneys, caves, or under roofs. The birds build their nests mainly of twigs and dry grass, all glued together with their saliva. The females lay two or three eggs, which hatch in 20 days. Right from the start, the parents catch insects in midair and feed them to their chicks. Since the parents are away for lengths of time catching insects, helper swifts care for the chicks while the parents are gone.

Tapir babies escape danger by staying close to their mother. Often, the newborn tapir cannot keep up with its mother, so she leaves it behind while she seeks fruit, berries, and leaves to eat. The calf's stripes help hide it on the sunny jungle floor. The mom comes back once or twice a day to nurse her baby. As the calf grows, the stripes fade and the baby learns how to find its own food.

#95 TAPIR CALVES ARE BORN WITH STRIPES

#96 TIGER CUBS WATCH AND LEARN

The female tiger gives birth to her two or three cubs in a secluded den. She raises the cubs with little or no help from the father. Around eight months of age, the mom starts teaching the cubs how to hunt and kill prey. Still, they stay with their mother until they are two or three years old. Mother tigers feed and protect their young from predators, yet few cubs survive.

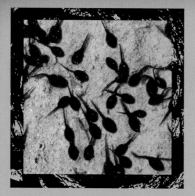

Female toads lay strings of tiny eggs on water plants. In a few days, the tadpoles, which look like small fish, hatch and swim in the lake or pond. About two months later, the tadpoles grow limbs and leave the water. Adult toads make their full-time homes in fields or gardens on land. They return to the water only when ready to lay eggs and produce the next generation of tadpoles. After that, they go back to the land.

#97 TOAD TADPOLES HATCH IN WATER

#98 TORTOISE HATCHLINGS HIDE IN THEIR SHELLS

Tortoises are like turtles, except that tortoises live on land and turtles usually live near water. Female tortoises dig nests in which they lay from 3 to 12 eggs. Both parents leave—and the eggs hatch in three to four months. The hatchlings break out of their eggs and dig their way out of the nest. But there are dogs, foxes, birds, and raccoons that can easily catch and eat them. The hatchlings' only defense is to pull in their heads and hide in their hard shells.

Weaverbirds usually make their nests by weaving together blades of grass and twigs. They hang their nests on tree branches, telephone poles, or on the tips of palm leaves. Some kinds of weaverbirds build small, individual nests that may have a long, narrow entrance to help keep out predators. Others, called social weaverbirds, build huge nests with as many as a hundred separate "apartments" under one giant roof.

#99 WEAVERBIRD CHICKS GROW IN HANGING NESTS

#100 WOLF PUPS LIVE IN PACKS

Most wolves are born in long underground tunnels called dens. The mother stays with the litter for the first few weeks as they feed on her milk. The father helps raise and care for the young, along with the rest of the pack of about 10 wolves. While the cubs still drink mother's milk, they start to eat chewed meat that the adults bring back for them. By four months, they eat only meat and hunt with the pack.

Foals can stand and walk soon after they're born, which helps them flee from lions and other enemies. A family group of zebras is made up of a male zebra, several females, and their young. The mother keeps the foal close to her while it is nursing. They also must learn to recognize each other's voice and smell. Only then does the mom let the dad and other zebras come near.

#101 ZEBRA FOALS CAN FLEE PREDATORS

INDEX

PHOTO CREDITS

Front Cover: leopard: Eric Isselée/Shutterstock; bonobo: Eric Isselée/Shutterstock; elephant: Steve Bower/Shutterstock; giraffe: JulijaSapic_Portfolio/Shutterstock; rabbit: Igor Klimov/Shutterstock; seal pup: Vladimir Melnik/Shutterstock; joey: K.A. Willis/Shutterstock; bear: Geoffrey Kuchera/Shutterstock; Chihuahua: Scorpp/Shutterstock; bird feathers: B & T Media Group Inc./Shutterstock; duckling: Eric Isselée/Shutterstock; giraffe spots: val lawless/Shutterstock; lion: Eric Isselée/Shutterstock; duck, flowers: sevenke/Shutterstock; polar bear: Eric Isselée/Shutterstock; cat: Utekhina Anna/Shutterstock; racoon: Becky Sheridan/Shutterstock; tiger hide: Anan Kaewkhammul/Shutterstock; pig: Volodymyr Burdiak/Shutterstock; **Back Cover:** axolotl: dezignor/Shutterstock; jackal: john michael evan potter/Shutterstock; chameleon: Lipowski Milan/Shutterstock; elephant: My Good Images/Shutterstock; sloth: Matthew W Keefe/Shutterstock; fox: Eduard Kyslynskyy/Shutterstock; ostrich: ChubarovY/Shutterstock; catfish: Stuart Westmorland/Design Pics/Corbis; **Interior:** 4b: C.C. Lockwood/Animals Animals; 4t: Associated Press; 5b: Associated Press; 5t: Danita Delimont/Alamy; 6t: blickwinkel/Alamy; 6b: epa European Pressphoto Agency creative account/Alamy; 7t: James Hager/Getty Images; 7b: iStockphoto/Thinkstock; 8t: Photoshot Holdings Ltd/Alamy; 8b: Cynthia Kidwell/Shutterstock; 9b: George Grall/Getty Images; 9t: Associated Press; 10t: Geoffrey Kuchera/Shutterstock; 10b: Tony Campbell/Shutterstock; 11t: Morales/AgeFotostock; 11b: Associated Press; 12t: 44kmos/Dreamstime; 12b: Christopher Meder/Shutterstock; 13t: Associated Press; 13b: ZSSD/Getty Images; 14t: Cathy Keifer/Shutterstock; 14b: NATURE'S IMAGES/SCIENCE PHOTO LIBRARY; 15b: Zoomteam/Dreamstime; 15t: Orhan Cam/Shutterstock; 16t: Lipowski Milan/Shutterstock; 16b: iStockphoto; 17t: Sue McDonald/Shutterstock; 17b: Anneka/Shutterstock; 18b: Kristof Degreef/Shutterstock; 18t: Associated Press; 19b: iStockphoto; 19t: blickwinkel/Alamy; 20t: Design Pics/Thinkstock; 20b: Gerard Lacz/Animals Animals; 21t: Associated Press; 21b: Outdoorlife/Dreamstime; 22t: Associated Press; 22b: Antares614/Dreamstime; 23b: blickwinkel/Alamy; 23t: FLPA/Alamy; 24t: iStockphoto/Thinkstock; 24b: Cynthia Kidwell/Shutterstock; 25t: Stephen Coburn; 25b: Anneka/Shutterstock; 26b: Alesik/Dreamstime; 26t: Larry Westberg/Shutterstock; 27t: Wild & Natural/Animals Animals; 27b: Mircea BEZERGHEANU/Shutterstock; 28t: iStockphoto/Thinkstock; 28b: Koletvinov/Dreamstime; 29t: Cullenphotos/Dreamstime; 29b: Number One/Shutterstock; 30t: D. Parer & E. Parer-Cook/Auscape/Minden Pictures/Corbis; 30b: Associated Press; 31t: Steve Bower/Shutterstock; 31b: iStockphoto/Thinkstock;

32t: Isselée/Dreamstime; 32b: Jami Tarris/ Getty Images; 33t: iStockphoto/Thinkstock; 33b: Associated Press; 34b: Brian Ardel/ SeaPics.com; 34t: blickwinkel/Alamy; 35t: blickwinkel/Alamy; 35b: john michael evan potter/Shutterstock; 36t: Tom Uhlman/ Alamy; 36b: iStockphoto/Thinkstock; 37b: Julija Sapic/Shutterstock; 37t: Jenny Sturm/ Shutterstock; 38t: iStockphoto; 38b: Anneka/Shutterstock; 39b: Roberto Pfeil/ AP/Corbis; 39t: Eric Gevaert/Shutterstock; 40t: SALLY MCCRAE KUYPER/SCIENCE PHOTO LIBRARY; 40b: James H Robinson/ Getty Images; 41b: Anettphoto/Dreamstime; 41t: Simone van den Berg/Shutterstock; 42t: iStockphoto; 42b: H Pieper/AgeFotostock; 43t: Anthony Mercieca/Animals Animals; 43b: Brenda Carson/Shutterstock; 44b: Tim Laman/Naturepl; 44t: PictureNature/ NHPA/Photoshot; 45t: Zuzule/Shutterstock; 45b: Maryart/Dreamstime; 46t: Satara910/ Dreamstime; 46b: Theijs Christian/ Shutterstock; 47b: Studio Carlo Dani/Animals Animals; 47t: iStockphoto; 48t: Neal Cooper/ Shutterstock; 48b: Solena432/Dreamstime; 49b: Hedrus/Shutterstock; 49t: CLEM HAAGNER/SCIENCE PHOTO LIBRARY; 50t: Naturesports/Dreamstime; 50b: Images & Stories/Alamy; 51t: Timhesterphotography/ Dreamstime; 51b: ght: electra/Shutterstock; 52t: Hotshotsworldwide/Dreamstime; 52b: iStockphoto; 53t: Michael Pitts/Naturepl; 53b: Associated Press; 54t: Associated Press; 54b: Photoshot; 55t: Kwiktor/ Dreamstime; 55b: Victoria Hillman; 56b: Greg3006/Dreamstime; 56t: Dmitriy Kuzmichev/Shutterstock; 57t: iStockphoto; 57b: iStockphoto; 58t: Associated Press; 58b: Tinka/Dreamstime; 59b: iStockphoto; 59t: Ingrid Curry/Shutterstock; 60t: Jaroslav74/Dreamstime; 60b: TOM MCHUGH/SCIENCE PHOTO LIBRARY; 61b: Dante Fenolio/Getty Images; 61t: Brandon Cole Marine Photography/Alamy; 62t: Heiko Kiera/Shutterstock; 62b: KEN M. HIGHFILL/SCIENCE PHOTO LIBRARY; 63t: Eric Gevaert/Shutterstock; 63b: i359702/Shutterstock; 64b: Images of Africa Photobank/Alamy; 64t: ChubarovY/ Shutterstock; 65b: Gregory K Scott/ Getty Images; 65t: Danita Delimont/ Alamy; 66b: Perry Harmon/Shutterstock; 66t: GMH Photography/Shutterstock; 67b: Kitch/Dreamstime; 67t: iStockphoto; 68b: Clarence Alford/Fotolia; 68t: iStockphoto; 69t: Associated Press; 69b: Associated Press; 70t: Gentoomultimedia/ Dreamstime; 70b: Fuse/Thinkstock; 71t: Zoonar/Thinkstock; 71b: Volodymyr Burdiak/ Shutterstock; 72t: Raycheu/Dreamstime; 72b: iStockphoto; 73b: AFP/Getty Images; 73t: Jean-Philippe Varin/Science Source; 74b: Christopher Wood/Shutterstock; 74t: Igor Kovalchuk/Shutterstock; 75b: outdoorsman/Shutterstock; 75t: LINDA FRESHWATERS ARNDT/SCIENCE PHOTO LIBRARY; 76t: Henk Bentlage/ Shutterstock; 76b: TOM MCHUGH/SCIENCE PHOTO LIBRARY; 77b: FLPA/Mike Jones/ AgeFotostock; 77t: Maksimilian/Shutterstock; 78t: Oxford Scientific/Getty Images; 78b: blickwinkel/Alamy; 79b: iStockphoto; 79t: Anikakodydkova/Shutterstock; 80b: Gerald A. DeBoer/Shutterstock; 80t: Becky Sheridan/Shutterstock; 81b: iStockphoto/ Thinkstock; 81t: iStockphoto; 82b: Fouroaks/ Dramstime; 82t: Colin Downs/Alamy; 83b: Christtophe Courteau/Naturepl; 83t: FRIEDRICHSMEIER/Alamy; 84t: jo Crebbin/ Shutterstock; 84b: bierchen/Shutterstock; 85b: Cornforth Images/Alamy; 85t: Kirsten Wahlquist/Shutterstock; 86b: Foryouinf/ Dreamstime; 86t: Beltsazar/Dreamstime; 87b: Rudie Kuiter/SeaPics.com; 87t: Papilio/ Alamy; 88t: iStockphoto/Thinkstock; 88b: Bjorn Stefanson/Shutterstock; 89t: